551   11259

The Earth

THE EARTH

Curriculum Consultants

Dr. Arnold L. Willems
Associate Professor of Curriculum and Instruction
The University of Wyoming

Dr. Gerald W. Thompson
Associate Professor
Social Studies Education
Old Dominion University

Dr. Dale Rice
Associate Professor
Department of Elementary and Early Childhood Education
University of South Alabama

Dr. Fred Finley
Assistant Professor of Science Education
University of Wisconsin

Subject Area Consultants

Astronomy
Robert Burnham
Associate Editor
Astronomy Magazine and *Odyssey* Magazine

Geology
Dr. Norman P. Lasca
Professor of Geology
University of Wisconsin — Milwaukee

Oceanography
William MacLeish
Editor
Oceanus Magazine

Paleontology
Linda West
Dinosaur National Monument
Jensen, Utah

Physiology
Kirk Hogan, M.D.
Madison, Wisconsin

Sociology/Anthropology
Dr. Arnold Willems
Associate Professor of Curriculum and Instruction
College of Education
University of Wyoming

Technology
Dr. Robert T. Balmer
Professor of Mechanical Engineering
University of Wisconsin — Milwaukee

Transportation
James A. Knowles
Division of Transportation
Smithsonian Institution

Irving Birnbaum
Air and Space Museum
Smithsonian Institution

Donald Berkebile
Division of Transportation
Smithsonian Institution

Zoology
Dr. Carroll R. Norden
Professor of Zoology
University of Wisconsin —
  Milwaukee

Managing editor
Patricia Daniels

Editors
Herta Breiter
Darlene Shinozaki Kuhnke

Patricia Laughlin
Norman Mysliwiec

Designers
Faulkner/Marks

Jane Palecek

Artists
Gill Embleton
Dan Escott
Elizabeth Graham-Yool
Illustra
Eric Jewell

Ben Manchip
Stephanie Manchip
John Marshall
Ray Turvey
Mike Whelply

First published by Macmillan Publishers Limited, 1979
Illustrations copyright © Macmillan Publishers Limited
  and Raintree Publishers Inc.
Text copyright © 1981 Raintree Publishers Inc.

Library of Congress Number: 80-22952
1 2 3 4 5 6 7 8 9 84 83 82 81
Printed and bound in the United States of America.

Library of Congress Cataloging in Publication Data
Main entry under title:

Let's discover the Earth.

  (Lets discover ;)
  Bibliography: p. 68
  Includes index.
  SUMMARY: A reference book dealing with the earth,
its atmosphere and weather, geology, volcanoes,
earthquakes, mountains, lakes, and other geographical
features.
  1. Earth — Juvenile literature. 2. Physical
geography — Juvenile literature. [1. Earth.
2. Geography] I. Title: Earth. II. Series.
AG6.L43   [GB58]   031s   [551]   80-22952
ISBN 0-8172-1760-6

LET'S DISCOVER
THE EARTH

RAINTREE PUBLISHERS
Milwaukee • Toronto • Melbourne • London

Contents

PLANET EARTH

The earth we live on is a large ball of rock. It moves around the sun. This picture shows what the earth looks like from the moon. The white part is clouds in the air around the earth. The air is the atmosphere.

The turning earth

As the earth moves around the sun, it spins like a top. The earth turns around once every 24 hours. When the place where you live faces the sun, it is day. Day becomes night as the place where you live turns away from the sun. It is darkest at midnight. That is when your place is facing directly away from the sun.

When it is midday in New York, it is midnight in Hong Kong.

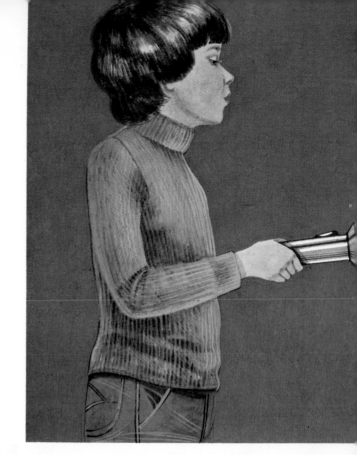

New York
midday

You can show how the earth moves from day to night. You can do this by shining a flashlight on a globe.

Pretend the flashlight is the sun. Mark where you live on the globe. Ask someone to turn the globe. You will see that when it is night where you live, it is day on the other side of the earth.

When it is midnight in New York, it is midday in Hong Kong.

New York
midnight

INSIDE THE EARTH

Suppose you could take the earth apart. You would find different layers inside. At the very center of the earth there is a core. It is made of solid metal. Around this core is an outer core of hot liquid metal. And around it all is a layer of rock called the mantle. The surface is the crust.

The core and mantle of the earth are thick. The crust is much thinner. The crust is like this thin layer of paint around the ball.

The earth's crust is thicker in some places than in others. Where it is very thick it sticks up above the level of the sea. We call these thick parts land.

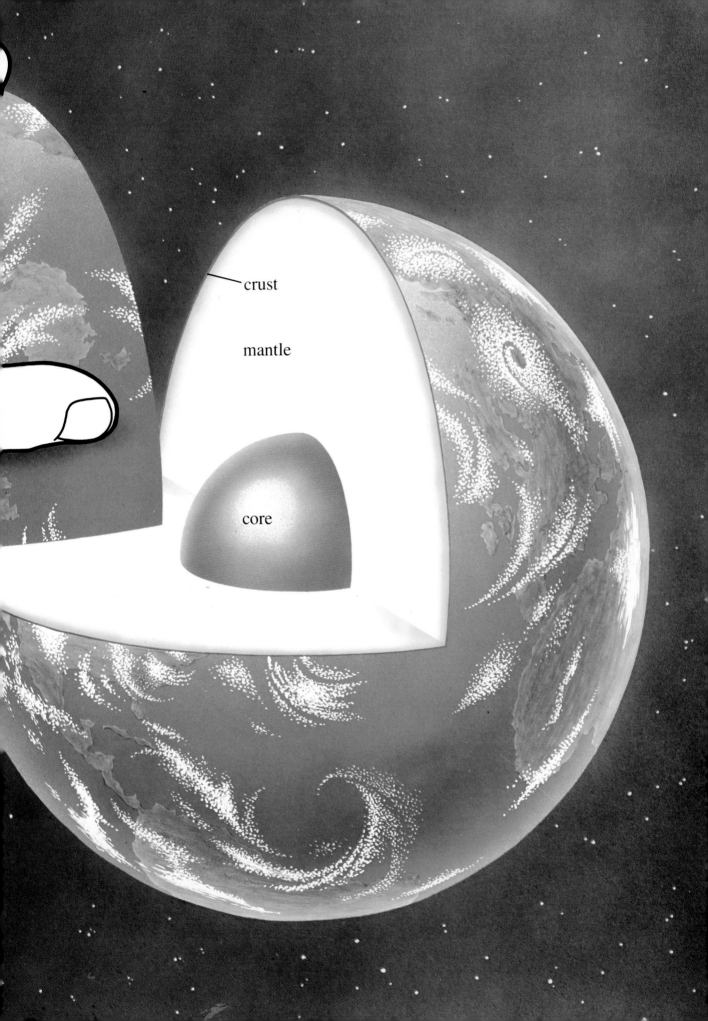

Earthquakes

Part of the mantle is made of hot, soft rock. This soft rock is always slowly moving under the earth's crust. This movement can make large cracks in the crust. Sometimes it makes one large piece of land slip against another piece of land. The ground shakes. This is an earthquake.

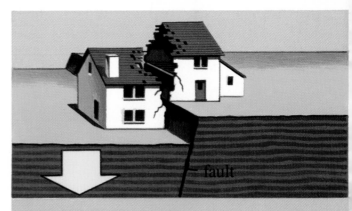

Sometimes a piece of land slips below the land next to it. The crack between the two pieces of land is called a fault.

At other times a piece of land slips sideways along a fault. The earth's crust has many faults.

In places where earthquakes may happen, low wooden houses are better than brick or stone houses. They do not fall down so easily. The picture at the left shows what a big earthquake did in Alaska. The shaking of the earth's crust made big cracks in the ground. Even wooden houses fell.

These tall buildings in Italy
were damaged by an earthquake.
Some of them collapsed into
piles of bricks and wood.

Volcanoes

Sometimes hot melted rock below the crust moves up to the surface. It is pushed out through a crack. It forms a volcano. A lot of gas in the melted rock pushes it upward. The gas explodes, and red hot rock pours out of the crack. This flowing rock is called lava. It piles up as it cools.

lava

This volcano formed in Iceland in 1973. Red hot lava shot high in the air. Bits of lava fell and buried some houses.

In the big picture, you can see the hot rock inside a volcano. Some lava is pouring out the top.

DAN ESCOTT 15

Rocks

Rocks are formed in many different ways. Basalt is a kind of hard lava. It comes from volcanoes. Shale is made from hard mud. Limestone is made from seashells. Shale and limestone formed at the bottom of the sea millions of years ago. Movements of the crust pushed them up as land.

This large statue in Egypt was cut out of sandstone. It was made thousands of years ago.

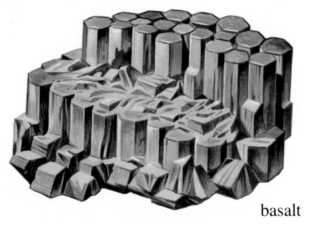

basalt

shale

These sandstone rocks were formed millions of years ago. They are made of sand grains stuck together.

limestone

This marble building is called the Parthenon. It is in Greece.
Marble is hard rock. It is used in many buildings. It is also used to make statues.

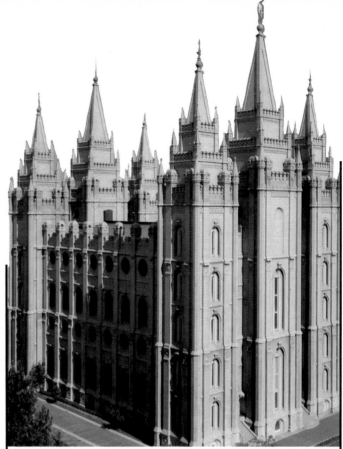

Granite is another very hard rock. This church is made of granite. It is in Salt Lake City, Utah.

Large pieces of marble are cut out of this hillside. Marble was formed from hot limestone inside the earth.

This is a granite pit. Granite formed millions of years ago. It formed from melted rock as it cooled slowly deep in the earth.

Minerals

The rocks of the earth's crust are made up of many different minerals. These pictures show a few of them and how they are used. Some minerals, such as diamonds and quartz, are made of many little pieces. These pieces are called crystals. Some are big enough to see.

diamonds

Diamond crystals are very hard. They are used to drill holes and as needles in record players.

bauxite

asbestos

Bauxite is a brown mineral. It contains aluminum. Aluminum is a useful light metal. Kettles and saucepans are often made of aluminum.

Asbestos crystals are long and thin. They do not burn. So asbestos is used to make fireproof clothes for firefighters.

gold

Each of the minerals in rocks formed in a different way. Diamonds formed deep in the earth's mantle. They came to the surface through cracks in the crust. Bauxite formed on the surface in hot and wet places. Quartz formed as hot melted rock cooled deep in the earth's crust.

Gold is a precious yellow metal. It has been used to make coins. Gold is very expensive because it is so hard to find.

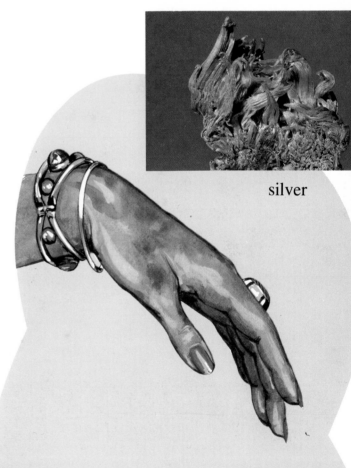
silver

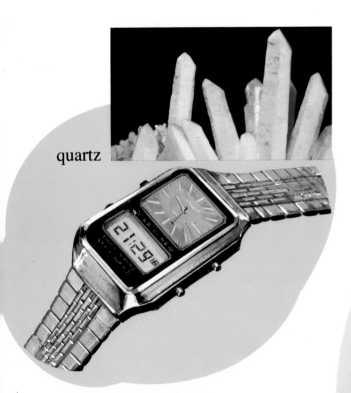
quartz

Quartz usually has long, clear crystals that are very big. They are used in clocks and watches to keep the time.

Silver is a precious metal. When it is polished, it is very shiny. It is used to make rings and bracelets and other jewelry.

19

Mining

Some rocks contain important metals. Such rocks are called ores. Other rocks contain layers of coal, salt, or asbestos. Digging for these things is called mining. Some ores or coal can be dug at the earth's surface. When ore or coal lies deep in the earth, it must be brought up.

The picture above shows a copper mine in Tasmania.

The picture at the right shows a coal mine. The people who work in the mine must have air to breathe. The arrows show how air moves in and out of the mine.

fresh air in

stale air out

People who work in mines are called miners. These two miners are digging coal. Coal is formed from plants that lived millions of years ago. The plants died and were buried in mud and sand. After a long, long time, they turned into coal.

In some places, tiny bits of gold can be found in streams. These people are looking for gold.

Oil

Oil was formed from tiny living things. This happened in the sea millions of years ago. When they died, their remains were squeezed and heated in the earth. After a long time, they turned into oil. People are using up the earth's oil very quickly.

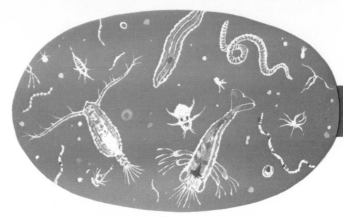

Tiny living things looked like this. They are drawn much bigger than they were.

The oil moves through the pipe to the shore. It is stored there in big tanks.

If there is enough oil, the ship lays a pipeline. It goes from the trap to the shore.

Later, the oil is pumped into a ship called a tanker. The tanker takes the oil to a refinery.

In the oil refinery, oil is separated into different kinds of oil products.

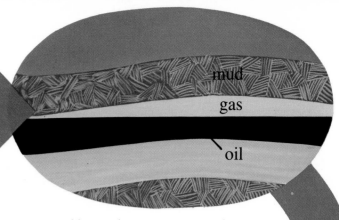

When they died, they sank to the sea floor and were buried. Much later, they turned into oil and gas.

The oil and gas moved upward. They were trapped under hard mud.

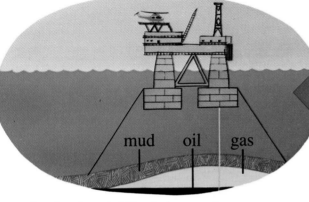

A hole is drilled into the sea floor to find out how much oil is trapped there.

Scientists in ships use special equipment to find oil that is trapped under the sea.

Some oil is refined into gasoline. Tank trucks take the gasoline to service stations.

At the service station, the gasoline is stored in tanks in the ground. Pumps put it into cars.

THE ATMOSPHERE

The atmosphere is a layer of air around the earth. Air is made up of different gases. Oxygen and water vapor are two of them. As you go higher in the atmosphere you will find less air. You will find it hard to breathe. People who climb high mountains take along extra oxygen. The oxygen helps them breathe where there is less air. This picture shows how high birds and airplanes can go.

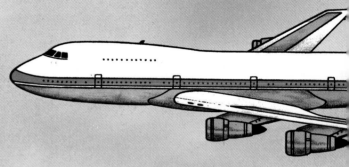

jumbo jet 15,000 meters
(49,200 ft)

light airplane 6,000 meters
(19,680 ft)

eagle 4,000 meters
(13,120 ft)

helicopter
3,000 meters
(9,840 ft)

highest
building
550 meters
(1,804 ft)

sea
level

Concorde 18,000 meters
(59,040 ft)

highest mountain 8,800 meters
(28,864 ft)

climbers

The water cycle

The sun warms the sea. This changes the top layer of water into water vapor. Vapor is a gas. The water vapor rises into the atmosphere.

water vapor

DAN ESCOTT

High up in the atmosphere it is very cold. This cold air turns the water vapor back to drops of water. The drops fall to the ground as rain. Some rainwater runs into rivers. The rivers run into the sea. People store some of the water in tanks. They use it later. Some rain soaks into the ground.

reservoir

Wind

Air rises when it is warmed by the sun. Cold air moves in to take its place. This moving air is called the wind.

You cannot see the wind. But you can feel it push against you. It flies your kite. It pushes against it and holds it up.

Wind can be very useful. Sailing boats use wind to push them across water. Windmills can use wind for pumping water or for running machines. In the past, large windmills with sails were used to grind grain into flour. Such a windmill is shown in the picture.

A whirlwind is one that blows around and around pulling up dust and leaves. Some whirlwinds are strong enough to do damage. The whirling wind in this picture is a tornado. Some tornadoes can pick up a horse or cow from the ground.

Strong winds can break up trees. That is what happened to this one.

Clouds and rain

Clouds are made of drops of water or of ice crystals. The drops and crystals are so small they can float in the air. Sometimes these tiny drops come together to form larger drops. These drops fall to the ground as rain. The ice crystals grow into snowflakes.

cirrus

cumulus

stratus

cumulus

Cirrus clouds are like feathers. They form high in the sky. They mean that rain is coming.

Cumulus clouds are puffy on top but flat on the bottom. They can bring heavy rain storms.

Layers of low clouds are called stratus. They may bring a steady rain or drizzle.

snowflakes

Snow

Snow falls when it is very cold. A snowflake is made up of many tiny ice crystals. All snowflakes are shaped like little stars with six points. Each snowflake is different from every other snowflake. Those shown on these pages are drawn much bigger than they are.

The picture at the right shows a large pile of snow sliding down a mountain. This is called an avalanche.

snowflakes

These children are having fun in the snow. But snow is not always fun. It can stop trains and cars from running. The train in the picture has a plow that clears away snow that has piled up on the rails.

Thunderstorms and rainbows

Thunderstorms usually happen in hot weather. Thunder clouds are tall and dark at the bottom. A flash of lightning is a large spark of electricity. Thunder is the noise made by lightning. The Romans thought lightning was their god Jupiter's weapon. The god Vulcan made thunderbolts.

It is easy to tell how far away a lightning flash is. When you see the lightning flash, start counting the seconds.

Jupiter

Vulcan

Stop counting when you hear the thunder. Divide the number of seconds by three to get the distance of the flash in kilometers.

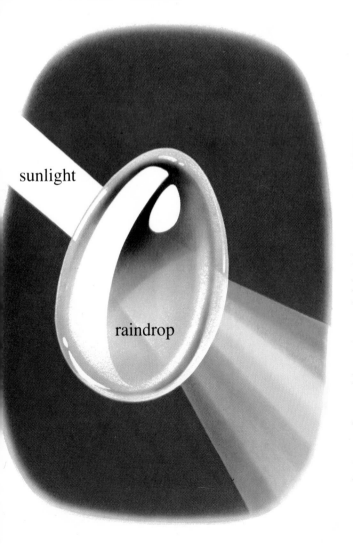

sunlight

raindrop

Rainbows are made when the sun shines on falling rain. The sun must be low in the sky to make a rainbow. Big raindrops give the brightest rainbows.

When it is both sunny and raining, raindrops act like millions of tiny curved mirrors. The drops separate the sunlight into different colors. You see these colors as a rainbow.

Watching the weather

It is fun to keep a record of the weather. Look at the sky each day. Are there any clouds? What kind are they? They may be high cirrus clouds. Or they may be puffy cumulus clouds. If the sky is gray all over, a low stratus cloud may be present.

To find out how warm or cold the air is, look at a thermometer outside.

You can make a chart to show what the weather is like each day. Draw a sun, a cloud, rain, or snowflakes on the chart.

Make a chart like this to show what the thermometer looked like.

To see how much rain falls in one day, catch the rain in a bottle with a funnel.

weather vane

Weather vanes point in the direction the wind is blowing from. If the wind changes direction, the vane will turn. You could make a weather vane. Use wood for the arrow and post. Cut the ends of the arrow from cards. Put a bead between the post and arrow. Join them with a nail.

The television weatherman uses weather records every day. Are they like your records?

Living in different climates

All over the world houses are different. That is because weather is different all over the world. In rainy places, houses have sloping roofs. The rain can run off of them easily. In hot, dry places, houses have flat roofs. In cold places, houses have thick walls to keep heat in.

Below are houses in Switzerland. They must be strong to stand up to snow, rain, and wind.

In part of West Africa, it rains a lot all year. The ground often is covered by water. The reed houses are built on poles to keep them above water. The roofs are sloping.

The picture below shows houses in another part of Africa. These houses are made of mud and have flat roofs. It does not rain often here. The people spend much time outside.

THE FACE OF
THE EARTH

For millions of years now, the earth's crust has been moving. This movement has pushed up land to form mountains. Water and ice slowly wear away the mountains. Streams and glaciers pick up tiny bits of rock and soil. They move these bits down the sides of mountains and carry them to sea.

glacier

hills

lake

cliff

cave

mountains

valley

island

stream

waterfall

sand

river

bay

shingle

Mountains

These peaks are very famous. They are the Himalayan mountains of Asia. The peaks were left behind as glaciers wore away the rest of the rock. The highest peak in the world is here. It is Mount Everest.

Rivers and streams

Streams usually start high in mountains. There is plenty of rain and melting snow up there. As the stream flows downward, it joins other streams. Finally, it gets big enough to be called a river.

The stream in the picture at the right is fed by snow water.

The river on the right is flowing through a deep gorge. The dam across the gorge uses the river's motion to make electricity.

Below is the River Rhine. It begins high in the Swiss mountains. It passes through Germany on its way to the sea. Boats carry loads up and down the Rhine.

River Rhine

Lakes and waterfalls

A lake is a hollow filled with water. Sometimes the hollow is the top of an old volcano. Sometimes the hollow is a valley made by a river or glacier.

The water in a lake often comes from a river. In other lakes, it comes from underground.

In Switzerland, there are many valleys with beautiful lakes like this one. Glaciers made these valleys thousands of years ago. When the ice melted, the valleys filled with water and became lakes.

When a river flows over a cliff, it forms a waterfall. As the water falls, it breaks up into a spray of little drops. Sometimes the spray wears away the side of the cliff, making a space behind the fall. In the picture, people are standing in such a space. They can keep dry there.

This big waterfall is in South America. The water drops nearly 1,000 meters (3,280 feet).

DIFFERENT LANDSCAPES

Most of the earth's rocks are covered by a thin layer of soil. Plants grow in this soil. What kind of plants grow depends on the weather. In warm, wet places, trees grow fast and form rain forests. In the Arctic, it is too cold for trees. Only small plants can live there.

In parts of Canada and Asia, winters are cold and snowy. There are forests of conifers. These are trees that have cones.

In many parts of the world there are large areas of grassland with few trees. The grass there may grow several meters (yards) high.

In some places, rain seldom falls. These places are called deserts. Few plants grow there.

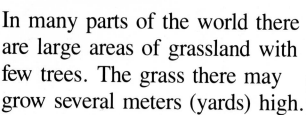

Far north in Canada there is thick ice that never melts.

Many parts of Europe and North America were once covered by forests. Now, most of the forests have been cut down. The land is used for farming.

equator

In parts of South America and West Africa near the equator, heavy rains fall all the year. There are thick jungles. Trees and other plants grow quickly.

49

The rain forests

Along the equator, the weather is usually hot and wet. It rains nearly every day. Trees grow quickly and form great rain forests. The tree tops are so close their branches rub together. Plants with long, thick stems climb around the trunks. The undergrowth is very dense.

The rain forest above is in South America. The picture was taken from an airplane. See how tall trees of many kinds grow very close together.

The women in this picture are working in a rice field in Japan. The rice grows in water in warm parts of the world. Heavy rains flood the land in summer.

Grasslands

In many flat lands far away from the sea, there is enough rain for grasses to grow. But trees cannot grow there. Wild animals once fed on these plains. Now sheep and cattle feed there.

The picture below shows a Masai herdsman and his cattle. They live in the high grassland of East Africa. The grass is thick because rain has just fallen.

These plants are all grasses. Emmer and einkorn grow wild. The others give us food.

corn   millet

emmer wheat einkorn barley

This is a plain in Hungary where wheat and corn are grown. The horses drink at a well.

A machine called a combine is often used to harvest wheat. The machine separates the grain from the straw.

combine

Hot deserts

Deserts are very dry places. Only a few kinds of plants and animals can live there. It is so hot at midday the animals must stay in the shade. At night it is cold.

scorpion

addax antelope

fennec fox

rattlesnake

gerbil

The picture below shows animals that can live in deserts. Scorpions and rattlesnakes look for their food during the day. Other animals hunt at night. At the left is the Sahara desert.

camels

pintail sand grouse

desert hedgehog

jerboa

ant lion

skink

Deciduous forests

The trees on these pages all have broad leaves. They are called deciduous trees. Most deciduous trees drop their leaves before the start of winter. They grow new leaves in spring. Many deciduous forests, such as the one at the right, have been cleared for farming.

birch

elm

horse chestnut

willow

ash

oak

Coniferous forests

The trees on these pages are all conifers. Conifers grow cones and have needle-shaped leaves. The leaves are tough. They can live in very cold and dry weather. Conifers often grow on cold mountains and in dry, sandy places. There are great coniferous forests in northern Canada, Europe, and Asia.

Scots pine

larch

cedar of Lebanon

Douglas fir

Each of these conifers grows
in a different part of the world.
Scots pines and Norway spruce
trees grow in northern Europe.
Redwoods and Douglas firs grow
near the west coast of North
America. Redwoods are the
tallest trees in the world. Some
are more than 100 meters
(328 ft) tall.

stone pine

blue spruce

redwood

Norway spruce

Tundra and ice

The land around the Arctic Ocean is called the tundra. It is too cold there for trees to grow. Only low plants such as moss and grass can grow there. They grow for a short time each summer when the frozen ground thaws.

The picture at the right shows what the tundra looks like during the short Arctic summer.

During the long, cold winter, this Arctic fox has thick white fur that keeps it warm. Its white color makes it hard to see in the snow. It lives in a hole.

When summer comes, the Arctic fox grows a new coat. This fur is short and brown. The brown coat is hard to see among the plants of the tundra.

This Eskimo hunter lives far north in Canada. He stands in front of part of an ice cap.

Spoiled land

This land was spoiled by waste from mining and rubbish from factories. Not many plants or animals could live here. Then the land was cleared up. Trees and grass were planted. The land was turned into a golf course. Spoiled land can be saved.

GLOSSARY

These words are defined the way they are used in the book.

aluminum (uh LOO muh nuhm) a very light, silver-colored metal

Arctic (AHRK tihk) the area around the North Pole that is always cold

asbestos (as BEHS tuhs) a mineral made of long, thin crystals that will not burn

atmosphere (AT muhs feer) the air around the earth.

avalanche (A vuh lanch) a sudden flow of snow, ice, earth or rocks down a mountain slope

basalt (BAS awlt) a hard, dark-colored rock made from cooled lava

bauxite (BAWKS yt) a brown mineral that contains aluminum

cave (kayv) a hollowed out space in the earth that is large enough for a person to enter

cirrus (SIHR uhs) clouds that are light and feathery and very high in the sky

cliff (klihf) an overhanging face of rock, earth or ice

climate (KLY mat) the average weather for a place

cloud (kloud) a mass of tiny drops of water or ice crystals that float in the air

coal (kohl) a black or brown ore used as a fuel

combine (KAHM byn) a machine that gathers grain from the field and separates the seed from the straw

coniferous tree (CON ihf uhr uhs tree) a tree that grows cones and needle-shaped leaves that last all year

copper (KAHP uhr) a common red metal

core (kawr) the central or deepest part of anything

crust (kruhst) the hard outside part of the earth

crystal (KRIHST uhl) tiny pieces of minerals that make up rocks

cumulus (KYOO myoo luhs) clouds that are puffy on top but flat on the bottom

deciduous tree (duh SIHD yoo uhs tree) a tree with broad leaves that are dropped every autumn and grow back every spring

desert (DEHZ uhrt) a hot, dry sandy area of land

diamond (DY muhnd) a mineral made of very hard crystals

Douglas fir (DUHG luhs fur) a coniferous tree that grows on the west coast of North America

earth (uhrth) the planet we live on

earthquake (UHRTH kwayk) a shaking of the ground

einkorn (YN kawrn) a type of wild grass

emmer (EHM uhr) a hard, red grain

equator (ee KWAYT uhr) the middle part of the earth where it is very hot and wet all the time

Eskimo (EHS kuh moh) a group of people who live in the Arctic

fault (fawlt) the crack in the earth's surface after two pieces of land slip apart

gasoline (GAS ul leen) a fuel that is made from oil

glacier (GLAY shuhr) a large mass of ice

globe (glohb) a round ball with a map of the earth on it

gold (gohld) a precious yellow metal used to make coins and jewelry

gorge (gawrj) a deep, narrow valley

granite (GRAN uht) a very hard rock made from melted rock that cooled slowly deep inside the earth

grassland (GRAS land) land with grass but no trees growing

Himalayan (hihm uh LAY uhn) very high mountains found in Asia

jungle (JUHN guhl) a hot forest where it rains all year

lava (LA va) hot flowing rock

lightning (LYT nihng) a large spark of electricity in the sky

limestone (LYM stohn) a rock made from seashells at the bottom of the sea

mantle (MAN t'l) a layer of rock surrounding the earth's core

marble (MAHR buhl) a hard rock made from hot limestone that was squeezed inside the earth

Masai (mah SY) a group of people that live in the grasslands of East Africa

midday (MIHD day) the middle part of the daylight hours

midnight (MIHD nyt) the middle part of the night hours

miner (MYN ur) a person who works in a mine

mineral (MIHN uhr uhl) a substance that is found in rocks

mining (MYN ihng) digging for ores

moon (moon) a heavenly body that circles the earth from west to east every 29½ days

mountain (MOWNT uhn) a large mass of land that is higher than the surrounding area

Mount Everest (mownt EH vur uhst) the highest mountain in the world

Norway spruce (NOHR way

sproos) a coniferous tree that grows in northern Europe

oil (oyl) a greasy liquid that will dissolve in alcohol but not in water

ore (awr) a rock that contains important minerals

oxygen (AWK sih jihn) a gas that has no color or taste and is found in air

Parthenon (PAWR thuh nawn) a marble building built in Greece a long time ago

pipeline (PYP lyn) a long, round object used to carry a liquid or gas over a long distance

plain (playn) flat ground that is often used as farmland

pump (puhmp) a device that moves liquids or gases from one area to another

quartz (kwarts) a mineral made of long, clear crystals

rainbow (RAYN boh) an arc of colored light seen in the sky

rain forest (RAYN fawr ihst) thick, wet forests that grow in the area of the equator

rattlesnake (RAT 'l snayk) a poisonous snake with a number of horny rings on its tail that makes a rattling noise when shaken

redwood (REHD wud) a coniferous tree that is the tallest in the world and grows on the west coast of North America

reed house (REED hows) a house built on poles to keep it above water

refinery (reh FY nuh ree) a place where oil is separated into different kinds of oil products

reservoir (REHZ uhr vwahr) a place used to store water

Rhine (ryn) a large river in Europe

Sahara (suh HAHR uh) a large desert in West Africa

sandstone (SAND stohn) a rock that was formed millions of years ago by grains of sand sticking together

scientist (SY uhn tihst) a person who knows a great deal about some branch of science

scorpion (SKAWR pee uhn) a small animal with claws like a lobster and a poisonous sting on its tail

Scots pine (SKAWTS pyn) a coniferous tree that grows in northern Europe

shale (shayl) a rock made from hard mud

silver (SIHL vuhr) a white, precious metal that can be polished and is often used to make jewelry

snowflake (SNOH flayk) a group of ice crystals that forms a pattern

stalactite (stuh LAK tyt) a tall pillar of limestone that grows down from a cave roof

stalagmite (stuh LAG myt) a tall pillar of limestone that grows up from a cave floor

statue (STACH oo) a likeness of a person or animal that is made from a hard substance

stratus (STRAT uhs) layers of low clouds

stream (streem) a flow of water that usually starts high in the mountains

tanker (TAN kuhr) a large ship used to carry liquids in large quantities

thermometer (thuhr MAHM eh tuhr) a device to measure temperature

thunder (THUHN duhr) the loud rumbling or crackling sound that follows lightning

tornado (tawr NAY doh) a dark column of wind that whirls around at a very high speed

tundra (TUHN druh) a treeless plain in the arctic region

vapor (VAY puhr) a gas

volcano (vohl KAY noh) a crack in the earth's surface through which hot melted rock pushes through

waterfall (WAW tuhr fawl) a flow of water falling from a high place

weatherman (WETH uhr man) a person who records and reports the weather everyday

weather vane (WEHTH uhr vayn) a device that is moved by the wind

whirlwind (HWUHRL wihnd) a wind that blows around and around

windmill (WIHND mihl) a device that uses wind to pump water or run machines

FURTHER READING

Adler, Irving and Ruth Adler. *Rivers*. Reason Why Series. New York: John Day Company, 1961.

Asimov, Isaac. *The Double Planet*. New York: Abelard-Schuman, 1966. 159pp.

Asimov, Isaac. *How Did We Find Out The Earth Is Round?* New York: Walker, 1973. 59pp.

Barnett, Lincoln. *The Wonders of Life on Earth*. New York: Golden Press, 1960. 216pp.

Barnett, Lincoln. *The World We Live In*. New York: Golden Press, 1956. 216pp.

Berger, Melvin. *The National Weather Service*. New York: John Day Company, 1971. 124pp.

Branley, Franklyn M. *The Beginning of the Earth*. New York: Crowell, 1972. 33pp.

Branley, Franklyn M. *A Book of Planet Earth for You*. New York: Crowell, 1975. 89pp.

Branley, Franklyn M. *Shakes, Quakes, and Shifts: Earth Tectonics*. New York: Crowell, 1974. 33pp.

Carona, Philip B. *Earth Through the Ages*. Chicago: Follett Publishing Company, 1968. 31pp.

Dayton, Mona. *Earth and Sky*. New York: Harper and Row, 1969.

Farb, Peter. *Ecology*. Life-Nature Series. New York: Time-Life, Inc. 1970.

Gans, Roma. *Caves*. Let's Read and Find Out Science Book Series. New York: Crowell, 1977.

Goetz, Delia. *Lakes*. New York: Morrow, 1973.

Goetz, Delia. *Mountains*. New York: Morrow, 1962.

Goetz, Delia. *Rivers*. New York: Morrow, 1969.

Heintze, Carl. *The Biosphere: Earth, Air, Fire and Water*. Nashville, Tennessee: Nelson, 1977. 128pp.

Hoke, John. *Ecology*. New York: F. Watts, 1977.

Kerrod, Robin. *Rocks and Minerals*. New York: Warwick Press, 1978. 44pp.

Knight, David C. *Let's Find Out About Earth*. New York: F. Watts, 1975. 40pp.

Lambert, David. *Earth and Space*. New York: F. Watts, 1979.

Lauber, Patricia. *This Restless Earth*. New York: Random House, 1970. 129pp.

Matthews, William H. *Earth's Crust*. New York: F. Watts, 1971.

Milne, Lorus and Margery Milne. *Mountains*. Life Nature Library. New York: Time-Life, Inc., 1970.

Olliver, Jane, ed. *The Living World*. New York: Warwick Press, 1976. 160pp.

Platt, Rutherford. *Worlds of Nature*. New York: Golden Press, 1962. 176pp.

The Raintree Illustrated Science Encyclopedia. 20 volumes. Milwaukee, Wisconsin: Raintree Publishers Limited, 1979.

Ryan, Martha. *Weather*. New York: F. Watts, 1976. 48pp.

Shuttlesworth, Dorothy E. *The Story of Rocks*. Garden City, New York: Doubleday, 1966. 57pp.

The World Book Encyclopedia. 22 volumes. Chicago: World Book-Childcraft International, Inc., 1980.

QUESTIONS TO THINK ABOUT

Planet Earth

Do you remember?

What is the shape of the earth?

What is the earth made of?

What does the word "atmosphere" mean?

In what two ways does the earth move?

How often does the earth turn around in 24 hours?

When is it day where you live?

When is it night where you live?

Find out about . . .

Time zones. How are maps marked to show time zones? In what time zone do you live? When it is noon where you live, what time is it in the time zone just east of your time zone? What time is it in the time zone just west of yours?

The earth and the calendar. Look at a calendar. How many times does the earth spin around on its axis in one week? How many times does it do this in the month of May?

Inside the Earth

Do you remember?

What is the inner core of the earth made of?

What is the outer core made of?

What is the earth's mantle?

What is an earthquake?

How is a volcano formed?

What is limestone made of?

Why is aluminum useful?

What do we get from mining the earth?

How was oil formed in the earth?

Find out about . . .

The San Andreas fault in California. How big is it? Is it safe to live near it? How was it formed?

Mt. St. Helens volcano. Where is it located? What kind of damage did it do when it erupted in 1980? Did scientists know it was going to erupt? Why were so many people killed?

The Atmosphere (1)

Do you remember?

What are two of the gases that make up the atmosphere called?

Why must mountain climbers carry oxygen?

What is the first step in the water cycle?

What happens to the rain that falls to earth?

What do we call moving air?

In what ways is the wind useful to people?

What is a tornado? What does it do?

Find out about . . .

Tornadoes. What causes tornadoes? When do
they happen most in the United States? What
general path do they follow? What can people
do to protect themselves from tornadoes?

How the oceans help the land. What happens
when the sun warms the sea? What part does
the movement of air play in helping the sea
bring water to the land?

The Atmosphere (2)

Do you remember?

What are clouds made of?

What do stratus clouds bring us?

What are snowflakes shaped like?

What is thunder?

What causes a rainbow?

What does a thermometer measure?

What does a weather vane tell us?

Why do houses in rainy places have sloping
roofs?

Find out about . . .

The work of meteorologists. People who study

the weather are called meteorologists. How do they learn about changes in weather before they happen? What instruments do they use? What do they learn from these instruments? How do weather maps help them?

Avalanches. What are they? Where do they happen the most? Why are they dangerous?

The Face of the Earth

Do you remember?

What do water and ice do to mountains?

What is the name of the highest mountain peak in the world?

Where do streams usually start?

How does a dam make use of a river's motion?

What is a lake?

Where might the water in a lake come from?

What causes a waterfall to form?

Find out about . . .

Stalactites and stalagmites. What are these structures? How are they formed? What are they made of? Where are they usually found?

Glaciers. When did great glaciers cover part of the North American continent? How far south did they reach? What did they do to mountains? What happened when the glaciers melted? What did they leave behind?

Different Landscapes (1)

Do you remember?

Where would you find the great rain forests of the world?

Why are there no trees in the Arctic?

What does a desert look like?

What is a conifer?

What does a jungle look like?

What is the machine called a combine used for?

Where do scorpions and rattlesnakes live?

Why do most desert animals come out to feed only at night?

Find out about . . .

Life in the desert. What kinds of plants live in deserts? What kinds of animals live there? How can these plants and animals stay alive in such a dry place?

Life in the rain forests. What kinds of plants and animals live in these forests? How often does it rain there? What do the animals do when it rains? How do the plants help the animals?

Different Landscapes (2)

Do you remember?

What does the word "deciduous" mean?

What happens to deciduous trees in spring?

The tough leaves of conifers have a special
    shape. What is this shape like?

What are the tallest trees in the world called?

What is the tundra?

What color is the Arctic fox in winter?

Why is the Arctic fox hard to see in the
    summer?

Where do Eskimos live?

Find out about . . .

How people are spoiling the land. What do
    industries do to spoil the land? What do
    people in cities and towns do to spoil parks
    and forest preserves? What can we do to stop
    spoiling the land?

How people live in jungles. What do they do to
    get food and water? What kinds of shelters do
    they have? Do they use the rivers and
    streams? How do they travel?

PROJECTS

Project — A Desert Landscape

Get an aquarium or a large box. Put some sand in the bottom. Now make a model of a desert landscape. Use modeling clay to make several animals that live in the desert. Using clay, bits of twigs, and small sticks, make models of plants that live in the desert. Place your plants in the sand. Then put your animals where you think they might like to be. You can find many pictures of desert plants and animals in books about deserts.

Project — Rain Forest Animals

Make a display of rain forest animals. First, look in an encyclopedia or in a book about rain forests for pictures of animals that live there. Make sketches of four animals that you like best. Then, using crayons, make drawings of these animals on thick paper or cardboard. Cut out your pictures. Color them on the other side. Then ask someone to help you make a small hole near the top of each picture. Tie a string through each hole. Hang your animals from a curtain rod in a window. This is your display of rain forest animals.

Project — A Deciduous Tree

Near the top of a piece of poster board, print the words "A Deciduous Tree." Then, using whatever colors you like, paint a picture of a deciduous tree in summer. Do this on the top half of your poster. Print under your picture the words "In Summer." On the bottom half of your poster, paint a picture of the same tree as it looks in winter. Print under the picture the words "In Winter." You can find pictures of deciduous trees in this book. Decide which one of them you want to paint. Think about how it would look in winter. Then paint the two pictures.

Project — Life in the Grasslands of Africa

Read all you can find about how zebras live in Africa. Find out about their enemies. Think about how the markings of the zebra's body make this animal easy to see in the dry, yellow grass in summer. Think about how the color of lions and tigers makes it easy for these animals to sneak up on zebras. Write a short story about a family of hungry zebras. Tell how they wait in the shade of trees at the edge of a grassy clearing. They are safe there from their enemies. The shade matches the stripes of their bodies. Then they decide to move into the sunlight to feed. What happens next?

INDEX

Photo Credits:
Aerofilms; B & C Alexander;
Heather Angel;
Australian News and Information Bureau;
J. Allan Cash; Robert Estall;
Michael Holford; Mats Wibe Lund Jr;
Photri; Picturepoint; R. K. Pilsbury;
Ronald Sheridan; Spectrum;
Swiss National Tourist Office;
John Topham; Zefa; Front cover: NASA